John F. Garvey

The Sounding Sea, and Other Poems

John F. Garvey

The Sounding Sea, and Other Poems

ISBN/EAN: 9783743335233

Manufactured in Europe, USA, Canada, Australia, Japa

Cover: Foto ©Thomas Meinert / pixelio.de

Manufactured and distributed by brebook publishing software
(www.brebook.com)

John F. Garvey

The Sounding Sea, and Other Poems

THE

SOUNDING SEA

.

- AND -

OTHER POEMS

- BY -

JOHN F. GARVEY

THE HICKS-JUDD CO.
PRINTERS, PUBLISHERS AND BOOKBINDERS
SAN FRANCISCO
-1896-

TO

THE UNKNOWN BARDS

WHOSE UNSELFISH DEVOTION TO THE MUSE

ARISES ABOVE ALL OBSTACLES OF TIME, PLACE AND SITUATION

I DEDICATE

THIS VOLUME OF POEMS

With Whatever Apologies Their Demerits May Demand.

CONTENTS.

PREFACE.

$\mathbf{I}$N publishing this first volume of poems, the author has no desire to trespass on the good nature of the public, or the charity of his friends. But he has no apology to offer, or ambition to shine for other than what he is. If crudities and defects are sought for, they will undoubtedly be found in plenty. The workmanship is, owing to uncontrolable circumstances, unfinished; nor are the themes classical. In common with his fellow-man he must submit to the demands of toil, which are resolute and unflinching. To the critic, the author has this to say: Knowing full well that poetry "gains little in those creeds which most find favor in the public eye," he hopes the fact may not prejudice them against an unknown versifier. Most likely they would resent any imputation on their sincerity— albeit such is not in anywise questioned. Yet, it cannot be gainsaid that an unheralded poet is a shining mark for satire's trenchant pen. By this, the author has no desire to forestall serious criticism; nothing is more foreign to his purpose. Nevertheless, he hopes these poems, or perhaps more properly called verses, may not be entirely in vain. But whatever is, is. 'Tis plain they contain many errors; which statement may prompt some to ask, why, then, did he publish? For reasons unknown to himself, but the winds may answer—he cannot. However, he is desirous of doing better. He may or may not succeed. Were he at liberty to pursue his bent, there might, at least, be some remote possibility of success. As it is, time, to which we must all become reconciled, can alone judge. Thuswise, and in this humor, he attempts to storm the citadels of conservatism, or as Tennyson would say, passes the Rubicon.

THE SOUNDING SEA.

The Sea! The Sea!—*Byron.*

Speak! though I tremble at thy voice;
Speak, mighty force! man doth rejoice
   To hear thee. If thou hast thy faults,
   Be not ashamed, though Rumor halts
To ridicule thy choice.

Sad sounding sea! the whispering wind
With apprehension is resigned;
   And surely from all envy void,
   Beholds thee consciously employed,
Soothing a sadder mind.

Oh! is it wrong that I should come,
To mock thee in thy cavern home,
   With simple song and rueful rhyme,
   Both slaves to custom born of time,
And both more burdensome?

Hath my devotion been too plain,
Too narrow, or too much for gain?
   Am I a child of fickle art,
   That I can never lose my heart
Without losing it in vain?

Despairing thus, I ofttimes lay
In silence, when to give thought play
   Were but a hollow, mocking show.
   Yet ever have I sought to know
What thou hast sought to say.

If this is wrong, I sin, and sin,
And will sin on until I win
    The utmost purpose of my will.
    Then only can my mind be still
And quiet reign within.

The dear, dead days that are not dead
Could testify to what I've said
    And what I never more may tell;
    Tho' unforgotten, 'tis as well
Their untimely thoughts have fled.

Their thousand secrets manifold,
That long hath smoldered in the gold
    And russet of departed years,
    Are new-awakened by the fears
Their memories unfold.

Yet, what a blessed thought it was,
Whose inspiration made me pause
    Beside thee; for I since learnt well,
    That nature hath great truths to tell,
In a most noble cause.

I saw the great sun lean its cheek
Upon a cloud, and to thee speak;
    And thereupon I did conceive,
    That charity would make thee grieve,
And pity make thee weak.

But no! the same indifferent air,
The some inhuman cast was there;
    Thy vaunted pride more manifest
    In that vague spirit of unrest
Which thou dost ever wear.

The fume, the fret, the tireless nod
Of courtesy—all passing odd,
   And very strange; one constant law;
   In all of which I ever saw
The handiwork of God.

To thee the silence of the Sphinx
Is nothing; or, at least, it sinks
   To nothing, measured with thy pride.
   What carest thou, in any tide,
What man or mortal thinks ?

Men call thee peaceful.   By what right?
The winds of the majestic night
   Echo no voice of thine that's fair;
   Magnificent thou art, but there
All beauty rests and light.

The earth, the air, the very sky,
And one all-penetrating eye,
   Are willing witnesses to this,
   For death, foul death, is in thy kiss,
And madness in thy sigh.

Therefore I love thee!   Be it just,
I know not.   Let it breed distrust,
   I care not.   This alone is plain :
   I love thee!   If I love in vain,
We do that which we must.

ADDRESS TO THE SONS OF EREBUS.

Vainglorious the deeds
That spring from cruel creeds
　　Of crafty men;
Glory nor marks, nor cares,
What garb dishonor wears,
　　Nor why, nor when.

It is enough to know
That Justice still will grow
　　And still endure;
Though something by that name
May credit her with shame,
　　She still is pure.

If lukewarm courage lives,
It nothing gains or gives
　　With civic pride ;
And like the scum of time,
Of reason, or of rhyme,
　　Must falsely guide.

Therefore, ye Sons of Night,
Like yon vast orbs of light,
　　Know first thy place!
Ye wage a fruitless war,
While these, thy late-born, are
　　A puny race.

Sooner self should forgive
The self that cannot live
　　Fair and discreet;
Sooner thou shouldst deny
The generating sigh
　　With each heart-beat.

A one-time noble fire
And patriotic ire
    Fast die away;
And conscience, to its shame,
Laughs, and the answer's lame,
    To pride's dismay.

But conscience not alone
Gives quarter, for ye own
    A deadlier foe:
Heart-selfishness with greed—
The insatiable seed—
    These, these ye sow.

They live, they bloom, they thrive;
Yet ever burn alive
    That which is good;
While ye that know the fact
Seem powerless to act
    When act ye should.

God gave you eyes to see;
God gave you liberty—
    This was to rule!
God gave you ears to hear
The true, the mighty seer,
    And scorn the fool.

God gave you discontent,
And spirit to resent
    Earth's present wrongs;
God gave you wisdom, brewed
In wisdom's solitude,
    From wisdom's songs.

Not force, but reason's lack
Gives, takes, and yet gives back
   What's ever thine.
Then why, O stubborn! why
This penetrating sigh,
   And great decline?

'Tis useless to deny
The art of sophistry
   And guarded speech;
Ye live, not what ye are,
But hide soft truth afar
   From mental reach—

Is envy's voice yet stilled?
Is poverty self-willed?
   Is judgment calm?
Is charity unjust,
That ye doth warrant trust
   And honor's arm?

Better the laws that live,
Fair and contributive
   To Reason's throne;
Better the light that failed,
If any spark prevailed,
   By force alone.

Honor means something more
Than strength to go before,
   And not offend;
Still something less, as well,
Which man lacks voice to tell
   Or comprehend.

All things live by thy voice—
Sufficiency and choice
　　And native grace;
And this rich, rolling earth
Gives noble prospects birth;
　　And time, and place.

Then rouse thy sullen hearts—
Those rigid counterparts
　　Of sin, not shame.
Let them with penance bleed,
Till Mammon's impure creed
　　Is lost to fame.

Since ye denied the Lord,
Turned penny-wise, abhorred
　　The true, the just,
There is no present peace,
Nor will thy yearnings cease,
　　Having no trust.

Know, therefore, what ye owe,
And if ye be so low
　　To scorn the debt,
Not for thyselves alone
Will the hereafter moan
　　With vain regret.

A race as yet unborn,
A race by ye foresworn
　　Before their time;
On them the stigma lies,
And likewise multiplies
　　And breeds the crime.

What think ye then of this?
What little can ye miss?
    Truly no grace.
There is more joy confined
In one pure, sinless mind
    Than *all* thy race.

Morose, ill-tempered Sons!
Thy span of life now runs
    O'er shallow beds;
While crafty knaves uphold
Bright, flaming swords of gold
    Above thy heads.

Be wise and grasp them not,
For they are keen and hot
    From Vulcan's forge.
They cut deep to the bone,
Nor skill can stay the groan
    Or bloody gorge.

But must ye still—still doubt?
Must Modesty cry out
    Her many wrongs?
Will no great sage arise,
And shame thy inbred lies
    With simple songs?

Oh! for the perfect day,
That comes and goes away,
    And leaves no sting!
Oh! for a mighty tide,
To swamp this hellish pride,
    And give truth swing!

Oh! for an uncoined word
To terrorize when heard,
  For ye are blind!
Oh! that ye may behold,
What blessings manifold
  Live undivined!

———

TO AN ORIOLE.

Stay, thou heavenly throated singer,
  Condescendingly awhile,
In the tree-tops linger, linger;
  Here is freedom, yonder guile.

'Tis the hour of silent sadness,
  Shrouded is the mind in gloom,
Let thy bubbling songs of gladness
  Ring where'er the cowslips bloom.

Listen! thy lone mate is calling,
  Watchful eye and woful heart.
Lo! the withered leaves are falling,
  Summer, Summer must depart.

Bird of promise, of unreason,
  Time is e'er a niggard knave,
Thou, the herald of the season,
  Know not why the days grow grave.

Sing, and may my thoughts grow lighter;
  Sing, the sun is on the wane;
Sing, for yon faint star grows brighter,
  And we may never meet again.

THE MUSE.

Like the stormy petrel winging
　O'er the wide, unfathomed sea,
Comes the echoes' constant ringing
Of the unknown voices, singing:
　She will love all else but thee!
She to whom thy soul is singing,
　She will love all else but thee!

Still the fields, the fields Elysian,
　Where immortal spirits dwell,
Haunt me like a ghostly vision,
Wavering between decision,
　Whispering—ah! pain to tell;
All unconscious of decision,
　Whispering—ah! pain to tell.

Picture of our phantom allies;
　Paint to nature, point to straw;
Votive of the flame that dallies
With the heart's vainglorious sallies,
　Bent to show the gaping flaw.
With the heart's spontaneous sallies
　Bent to show the gaping flaw.

Oft the misty clouds seem breaking,
　Hopeful sunshine bathes the lea;
Then the voices, unforsaking,
Bid me cease my undertaking,
　Saying, she will love not thee;
Cease a fruitless undertaking,
　She will love all else but thee.

Yet I love the ages hoary
　When she laved full many a brow;
May she live the noble glory
All, and all in all of story,
　And no barren claim allow.

IN POTTER'S FIELD.

Sweet mignonettes! sure ye were blest indeed,
   When left to bloom in these unhallowed grounds,
In fitting contrast to the haughty reed
   That scorns thee for thy birth in alien mounds;
Yet thou, ill-nurtured like an unkempt weed,
   Doth lovelier thrive where poverty abounds.

Ye purchased, true, a poor inheritance,
   Purchased, and yet paid nothing, nothing owed;
But with indifference thou dost advance
   Thy own small fortunes, whilst a heavy load
Is lifted from the eyes that look askance
   At man's ingratitude in this abode.

O hoary fate and furtherance of time!
   Thus consecrated are the years we shed.
What threnody can make their absence chime
   With this uncertainty?   Here, hope lies dead
And buried with the lives whose only crime
   Was to be better than the world they fled.

Let contrite ones drop participles here,
   And wither with the nature of the spot,
Marking a tension of unholy fear,
, For thus, unwitting may they be forgot
When life's contractions and an unspanned year
   Doth doom them to some likewise measured plot.

Love's glittering consummation, and the hope,
   Breathing the prescience of an argent light
That shines from heaven, may lose their crystal scope,
   And seem by retrospect a baneful blight
In this quadrature, whose lean arms doth ope
   To ush the heedless to eternal night.

Well may the moon and all too-purple sun
    In mutual pity burn their candles out;
For here, no monumental shadows run
    To leave a wonder, fashioned from a doubt;
Nor for a moment is the soul undone
    By spirits mighty, militant, devout.

Nay! nothing can afford the eye delight,
    Nor grace, nor symmetry indulge their kind;
Earth seems at variance with the woful sight
    That mars her famed escutcheons out of mind,
And humbles mortals with a darling spite,
    To bruit the failures humor hath designed.

The bluebird sings her melancholy song
    As if sweet music's tones were ill-bestowed;
Whilst nothing can her measured stay prolong
    Beyond one short and transitory ode;
But quickly flying hence proclaims the wrong
    That lies unsheltered in the public road.

O unjust man! to spite the living dead
    Why dost thou worm thy hatred to the grave?
With bare-faced calummy, oft hast thou said :
    That they who died left nothing time could save
To fame's delight.   Dwells there no shame, no dread,
    No honored crypts thou may'st hereafter crave?

Thou generous earth that coverest these bones,
    Let not the fates expose th' unguarded truth,
Nor foul-mouthed beasts with their discordant tones
    Mock homely sympathy and honest ruth
Of unforgetful maidenhood that owns
    The love of kindred or the friend of youth.

Such lone exceptions are, by heaven's grace,
  Pearls that are valued not by weight of gold
Or sacriligious bribes. They find a place
  Where honor is as sacred as of old;
Where chastity is written in the face,
  And simple sweetness scorns the ages bold.

Long service to the world's desire hath turned
  Our boasted pride to foulest villainy;
Wherein base selfishness hath deeply burned
  Its special stamp, and ev'ry eye may see
How little we with virtue are concerned,
  Though feigning love and whole-souled piety.

What equal lights our consciences demand
  Is nothing to the purpose or the will.
Platonic love and sin go hand in hand,
  And 'tis a verity, their creed will kill
The favorite flower of a favored land,
  Who prophesy what time cannot fulfil.

Oh, pause! ye merrymakers, pause awhile;
  ·Feigned gaiety mocks reverence withal;
Thy sires sleep uneasy in exile,
  And ye hath witnessed their degrading fall—
Aye! sold them into slavery by guile,
  Profaning death with this impious scrawl—

On yonder heights a mercer's body lies
  Beneath a sculptured sepulchre of art,
Whose granite concave cleaves the western skies,
  And craves distinction in each well-turned part;
Yet never he beheld with spirit eyes,
  An angel with forgiveness in her heart.

His life was one long pestilential curse,
  Wherein no tie was sacred to his love.
The orphan's plight, the widow's empty purse,
  Attest how his rapacious greed didst move
Desire within him ; yet the psalmer's verse
  Told how the seraphs welcomed him above.

Out on such infamy ! ye knew him well
  And with what charity he held thy cause—
Ye servant millions. Oh, what truth to tell,
  But where the tongue to utter it ! The laws
Were bent to serve his purpose, nor rebel
  Against the pressure of unjust applause.

Yet here behold the unmarked grave of one
  Who lived an honest man and nothing more.
But 'tis presumption to dilate upon
  The virtues his, the vices he forebore—
Unfortunate in fortune, and the sun
  Of his omnipotence is clouded o'er.

Bland spot, farewell ! Darkness veil thou mine eyes!
  And thou free wind from yon Pacific seas
Perform thy holy orisons ; nor rise,
  Reticent stars ; ye that didst whilom ease
Who sleep within. Let not their souls surmise
  That they in dying lived to thus displease.

THE VISION.

Land of the icy north,
  Land of the polar bear,
Stem thy tempestuous wroth;
  Base-born renown forswear.

Isle of the midland sea,
  Isle of the lukewarm wave,
Reared to immensity,
  Yield what thy birthright gave.

Mount of the golden shore,
  Shasta in white array,
False to thy milk-white floor,
  Tremble and mark this day.

Foil of the Arctic blast,
  Sweet semi-tropic zone,
Seek in thy largess vast
  Wonders as yet unknown.

Day of the fiery morn,
  Night of the starless pall,
Why dost thou not forewarn
  They who would tether all?

Harken! the universe
  Champs at its iron bit;
See how it doth disperse
  They who would temper it!

God! but the sculptured clay,
  Dumb as Amphion's bride,
Moves with impassioned sway;
  Feels all the hand denied.

Earth of the nether world,
  Brood thou with heavy care;
Worms in thy alcoves curled,
  Move with uneasy air.

King of the leaden heart,
  Queen of the purple throne,
Draw thy slow lids apart,
  Scoff and thou'lt scoff alone.

Man with the subtle soul,
  Stand and behold thy fate ;
List to the mournful dole
  From the proud-born of state.

Witness the pending clash,
  Death is the woful meed;
Note twixt the lightning flash,
  Bent of the blood-red reed.

Stem of the erring one,
  Where roams thy progeny ?
Hate which was cast upon
  Their heads returns to thee.

Drink from the wormwood cup,
  Bitter the taste, you vow ?
Oft hast thou filled it up,
  Filled, nor didst drink till now.

Lord, how the pregnant air
  Stifles with fearful stench ;
Black clouds with fraughtful care
  O'er yonder hills entrench.

Hark, now ! the deist's oath,
   Launched is to heavy space,
Hurled back with echoes' growth,
   Smites full the skeptic's face.

Slain in his beaten track;
   Black turns his body's wall;
Flee ! flee ! and look not back,
   Lot's fate may wait ye all.

Loud roars the savage beast,
   Short snaps the lion's tail,
Fierce for the coming feast—
   God, let thy will prevail !

Judgment hath come to pass:
   This, the eternal day,
Strikes dumb, alas ! alas !
   Hearts of unyielding clay.

False was the prophet's pray'r;
   False was his prophecy;
Earth's holy fanes the snare
   Where he enforced his fee.

Hush! hush! breathe nevermore.
   Die! die! and dead remain.
Farewell, retreating shore—
   Christ Child is born again.

Braw singer, ye hae wandered lang,
Frae Coila's heaths, where whilom rang
The merrie echoes o' thy sang
    In lays sae tunefu' ;
The lyre hae laist its master twang,
    An' bards grown runefu'.

The daisies i' the moorlan' pine,
An' a' the melancholy kine
Hae dootsum step an' dowie eyne
    Alang the field ;
While ilka day they fret an' whine
    Wi' wrinkled eild.

The golden starns blink i' the sky,
An' loe-lorn lassies aften sigh
Wi' tears encased i' ilka eye—
    Ah ! na vain habbie ;
E'en a' the little bairnies cry
    Fae sangs o' Rabbie.

Sae maun, I ken, ye dinna seek
To twitch the conscience o' th' weak,
But brawley, an' wi' patience meek,
    Wad aften gaze
I' pity on their sins, na speak
    O' blasted days.

Na hae they kend thy muse fae naught,
But found the rustic grace they sought
Amang thy leaves o' lear, fu' straught
    An' free o' guile ;
Nane winna doot what they hae brought
    An' pleased the while.

Ah ! well may ilka pilgrim pause
Beside the tomb that overawes,
An' teaches them the giftie's cause
    Twixt waefu' wheeze ;
Then steal awa' to gie applause
    Wi' moistened e'es.

Fu' mony hours sleeps the rose,
Afore the tented nursling blows ;
Yet sum dark nicht 'twill a' repose
    An' fade awa'
Frae this bleak warl o' muckle prose,
    Ilk luve's ain star.

An' if the ghaists o' simmer days
Dance lang whyle fulsum fancy plays
Her diverse tunes an' canny lays,
    What matters it ?
Maun 's seldom guid, that seldom weighs,
    A fruitfu' wit.

Wha winna reconcile the fair,
Wi' ilka mood o' wardly care,
If the puir heart is lacken there
    To gie us pleasure ;
An' ilk thysel' as aft despair
    Ayont a' measure.

Gin sonsy lassies fu' o' pride,
An' honest laddies lang denied,
Nae mair in looing bliss reside.
    Ane stubborn pen
May well forget thine able guide,
    But nae till then.

Though Scotia hae been charged wi' lack
O' ripened wit—sic vain attack
Frae spitefu' anes is hurl'ed back
  To they that gie it ;
Let pridefu' fools their numbskulls rack,
  Thy notes belee it.

Fae ye couldst sae unfauld a tale
To make the wanton deathly pale,
Or else provoke a hearty gale,
  O' honest laughter ;
Whyle I in simple sadness fail
  By smiling after.

'Tis thusly mortals winna see
How merit is divorced i' me ;
Yet downa I help framing thee
  In some rude verses,
E'en if they only bring as fee
  A critic's curses.

But deil-I-care; thy jigging tune
Hae led me to the " Bonnie Doon,"
Where aft I saw the golden moon
  Shine owre it ;
An' troth, I winna part fu' soon
  Frae sic a fit.

Mair ease to girnin, wizen'd maun,
Wha wi' a wat'ry e'e may con
The prosy work o' an' auld Don,
  Mair ease I say;
But happier I when dreaming on
  The fields o' Ayr.

The fause wi' pride are lappin' up
Wi' greedy aspect at each sup,
The doctored dregs frae folly's cup,
        To leave behind
A name at ilka stage corrup'
        An' unrefined.

Sic hath the guid in life became
Ill-sotted that our mither hame
Is a' agley, an' ilk the same
        Wha died awa';
But stirred the ashes o' luve's flame
        Wi' hell's ain paw.

An' aft methinks a'm owre lost
When by sic wheezlin' churls a'm crossed,
An' by their daein's tempest-tossed
        Frae space to earth;
But this airt naithing to thy cost
        Na social worth.

Aboon the yird, amang the skies,
Ye soarest where the proud yearn flies,
Frae ilka danger that belies
        Our warl below ;
Where each new year but amplifies
        The mony's woe.

An' ilk the clouds that's hurled apace
By simmer winds unto the chase
O' phantom faes that flood the space
        O' upper air ;
Thou dost sae fill my soul wi' grace,
        O' luve most fair.

'Tis not auld Scotia's doom tae dee
Frae cauld neglectit, na tae see
The banefu' haud o' calumny
    Laid on her urns ;
Fae she will ever live i' thee,
    Bold Rabbie Burns.

Sae now fareweel ! gie my respects
To a' the muse-inspired elects,
Wha living were the architects
    O' deathless sangs ;
Their clearer wisdom aft reflects
    These deeper wraugs.

IF SHE SHOULD DIE.

If she should die—O most unhappy day!
I would call thee unhappy in my lay.
  Though thou mightst not seem joyless on thy face,
  Yet inwardly methinks mine eye could trace
Something of sadness to thy own dismay.

Harp not on death, world-weary heart, I pray;
'Tis ill of thee.   Let others only say:
  It pleaseth God.   In me no joy hath place
    If she should die.

What skilful alchemist could then convey
To life the love that lives in voiceless clay ?
  Nothing of sweetness bred 'neath heaven's space,
  Nothing of woman nor of woman's grace,
But to whose charms I fain would answer: nay!
    If she should die.

LIZZIE.

O Life! that teemed with wondrous bliss,
  When Lizzie's hopes were young,
Where are thy joys which seemed to kiss
  The days that lived unsung?

The years were honest with themselves,
  And generous to me,
But now my spirit ever delves
  With their uncertainty.

For Lizzie, once the daylight's sun,
  Is listed with an age
That marks a gaping void upon
  An elsewise worthy page.

If she oft loved her lightsome mood,
  And I a mood of care,
Her gaiety was not the food
  To strengthen man's despair.

She oft was petulant, she'd own,
  Which guardedly I claimed,
Yet chastity hath in her grown
  To something higher famed.

Though prodigal in that which I,
  Mayhap, would welcome less;
Untempered, too, and nowise shy,
  Which these same traits confess.

Whene'er she owned a sin or two,
  'Twas I withheld the same,
Yet hers were simple ones and few,
  But mine—Oh, spare the name!

All her ripe qualities outweighed
   The thoughts that gave them birth;
Therefore her higher nature played
   A spotless role on earth.

However meant, she loved to doubt
   The sinfulness of me,
And this it was that drew her out
   To a minute degree.

But she was rich—Oh, rich in love!
   Which is of all things rare;
With what avail? The end thereof
   Is death, and death will dare

The pleasures of a happy girl,
   Whom nature called a sister,
And fate hath urned my priceless pearl
   Ere woman's sunshine kissed her.

Camellias now bloom o'er her grave,
   Pure as the fair soul hither,
And oft in autumn-time I crave
   A wish like them to wither.

Though these sweet messengers do tell
   That Lizzie is at peace,
Yet it were better I that fell
   Than her young life should cease.

No promise can the world-gods hold,
   No rest when cold stars glisten,
Her footsteps on the paths of gold
   Are sounds for which I listen.

Oh, would I knew their gentle fall
   And her melodious laughter!
Oh, would that she would deign to call,
   What matter what thereafter!

THE GREAT DESIDERATUM.

I must be sad when I have cause and smile at no man's jest.—*Shakespeare*.

Love rises to affluent heights,
    And hearts that love may joy therein;
Love is the queen of all delights,
    But sorrow is the sweetest sin.

Ask this of the immortal stars,
    And all their tongues of flame are dumb;
Ask yon bright orb that midway bars
    The light that is from that to come.

No answer, but a silent scorn;
    For there the naked truth is plain:
To ev'ry life is sorrow born
    Which comes and goes and comes again.

Then tell me not that this is this,
    Nor bid me find nepenthe here;
I only know that which I miss
    Was never to me less than dear;

Was never to me less than sweet;
    Was never to me less than fair;
Therefore I hold it fully meet
    If I should wither with despair.

Confine my sorrow and my wo
    With me, myself, the inner man,
But let my stricken shadow go
    Where'er it will, whene'er it can.

My influential star lies hid
    In yon vast field of native blue;
I know it ! for the grave's low bid
    Was higher than my life was true;

Nor yet so high that all my love
  Was conquered by an earthly storm.
The heart's great fulness is above
  The vanities of face and form.

And truth dares match itself with truth,
  When time with time is all concerned;
It must be, though the gods of youth
  Are ever dead, forever urned.

Then let me love and give my heart
  To she who hath no heart to give;
Let wisdom play its valiant part
  Where sorrow is designed to live.

Better to sign a bond with death,
  That nowise scorner of a knave,
Than own with treachery a breath
  That lies to make itself seem brave;

That lies to make itself seem gay
  When gaiety is not its friend;
If joy may fashion out its day
  Then sorrow too may not offend.

Not that a holocaust were made
  Of all the supreme bliss of earth;
Not that th' unwilling self were laid
  Where all things have a common birth.

But only a distinction drawn,
  And from the works of man apart,
When sorrow's penetrating thorn
  Wounds deep th' already wounded heart.

I say 'tis well who found it so—
  Afflictions have a just reward;
I say 'tis well, and then I know
  All things are but the work of God.

And He knows best that which is best
  For me or this soul part of me;
And am I not then doubly blest
  In knowing what I cannot see?

Were I a witness to the growth
  Of just a simple, lupin flower,
My faculties were nothing loth
  To rail against the God of power.

Because I cannot see, I feel
  There is a something hid from sight;
Because I cannot see, I kneel
  And pray to her who knew the right;

And pray to her who witnessed things
  Which were withheld from many men,
Whose scope is narrowed down to kings
  Of reason and of mortal ken.

For folly and the like of such
  She was not preordained a child;
Though truth, made plain by her soft touch,
  Is still by humankind reviled.

Yet reason and the reason given
  To she, inspired in her deeds,
Still lives, attracting souls to heaven
  That otherwise were sluggish weeds.

But lo ! this inward pulseless void
  Bears witness to a void without;
Her light, which I might have enjoyed,
  Is missing from a world of doubt.

Why is it thus?   Why should it be ?
  Why should her heav'n-born spirit fly ?
Earth's godless mortals thrive, but she,
  Whom Virtue loved, must pine and die.

What prophecy is in the deed?
  What hope hath blest its nature since ?
Where is the key to such a creed ?
  Oh, tell me God ! for I am dense ?

Oh, tell me God ! though I am base
  To question any act of Thine,
If I do sin and fall from grace,
  How much of it is sin of mine ?

Great Questioner of thoughtless man,
  Is there aught hope for such as I ? ˙
Am I foredoomed to live my span
  Forever and do naught but sigh ?

Forever distant from a soul
  With whom Thou did'st of late commune;
Fore'er disputing Time's control;
  Forever out of sense and tune.

The very essence and the sum
  Of all my love I freely give;
Yet life is lonely, cumbersome,
  In truth I am not fit to live.

In truth I am not fit to die,
   And wherefore may I then abide?
It matters not. If she is nigh
   My soul's one wish is not denied.

However man may be displeased
   To me 'tis nothing that I owe;
My own is mine; nor am I leased
   To dress my life for empty show.

The memory of what has been
   Will never change its bountied son;
And all things that are unforeseen
   May end as they have all begun.

Or leave their willing marks behind
   As outposts to posterity;
For that which is, is well designed,
   And that which is not, cannot be.

Thus from a seeming chaos born,
   Nowhere that any can divine,
May rise a glorious-lighted morn,
   Than any that hath yet been mine.

But even granting it, and so
   Presuming that the wish is dear,
This self-bound spirit will not know
   It is the day of all the year.

There is a victory in death,
   That victory it may not love,
Yet sings, too, with its latest breath
   For she who knew it will approve;

For she who knew it soon beheld
   The truth made practical and plain;
Alas! too soon, nor yet rebelled
   For she is happy in the gain.

And in the face of this despite,
   This great and counteracting ill,
Things are denied me which were light
   To my once unrestrain'ed will.

A quotient of the years to come,
   A resumè of years long dead,
Is little to the mighty sum
   Of burdens passing o'er my head.

Yet, notwithstanding it, the past,
   I can rehearse without a moan;
As if my yesterdays were cast
   In cold, imperishable stone.

Nor mine alone, but those of whom
   Words were not made to fitly speak;
Her innocence will oft find room
   To show the world why I am weak.

Though good-intentioned deeds seem vain,
   And well-conceiving words are crossed,
And sneering, carping wits complain,
   Yet all is not forever lost.

The present cannot hold the mind
   Inviolate to its own aim;
It must, it will soar to its kind,
   And that's the all of all I claim.

If then the arbiter of time
    Accuses me of selfish thought,
I own it, but it was no crime ;
    I own it, though it came unsought.

And I am thankful it is so,
    Since it hath thusly came to be;
What it may prove I do not know,
    Its punishment is sweet to me.

Man was not born in perfect grace—
    Perfection only dwells above ;
Nor can his any deed efface
    The immortality of love.

TO C. H.

Oft have I craved the wisdom of that bard
    Who listed in the Promethean ranks
    Unheralded; with it I could give thanks
In no ambiguous key.   Alas ! 'tis hard
When such unequal words my thoughts retard,
    And leaves me drifting like those mountebanks
    Of feudal times.   Yet my young pranks
I fain would never fully disregard;
They teach me, Clifford, in what proper light
    To look upon thee; and 'tis evident
I've squared the circle in my soul to-night
    By thy soft words and gentle argument.
But for thine aid, I were a slave to pelf—
You knew me better than I knew myself.

—JANUARY 5, 1891.

O JESSIE! WHEN THE DAY IS DONE.

O Jessie! when the day is done
  To thee my thoughts revert;
Their own true nature dwelleth on
  My own, my mortal hurt.

If once the brave deceives the fair,
  Must time still fly between
The household of an orphaned heir,
  Of love and love's demesne?

Forgive me, and the blessed deed
  Recorded in thy heart
Will level time and intercede
  For that which lacketh art.

The sins of reason and of rhyme
  Are not to me less base
Than that which thou dost hold a crime,
  And I would not efface.

Consider how and where and when
  I sinned at beauty's altar;
Consider, Oh, consider! then
  I know thou wilt not falter.

Forgiveness is a holy charm,
  Than truth, is nothing fairer.
Too late? 'tis ne'er too late for balm,
  And love's a known despairer.

The heavens, sweet, are listening,
  With hopeful eyes and damp;
The moon that late was glistening
  Turns low its ruddy lamp.

One word, and nature wakes again,
    One word of instant breath;
One word, one word, or its refrain,
    One word, one word, or—death.

———

THE FISHERMAN'S LAST FAREWELL.

Lo! a storm is on the sea,
        Lammermoor;
Meaning troubled hours for thee,
        Lammermoor;
But no longer vigils keep,
Nurse thy gentle soul to sleep,
And to-morrow thou may'st weep,
        Lammermoor.

Not a star is in the sky,
        Lammermoor;
Not a beacon-light is nigh,
        Lammermoor;
Life's long cherished hopes have fled,
And my future's with the dead,
And my grave the ocean-bed,
        Lammermoor.

Helpless drifts my little boat,
        Lammermoor;
Striving hard to keep afloat,
        Lammermoor;
Yet the loudly flapping sail
Cannot in the end prevail,
But I'll die and never quail,
        Lammermoor.

ODE TO DISAPPOINTMENT.

Unpitying wight! thy handiwork is here!
   What inward is, is outward in its action,
     Outward and upward, nothing daunting it—
From which arises a distempered fear
   Bordering on the realms of distraction;
     Merging to moods that are the least unfit,
When all the intense agony is o'er,
And hope's bright star is dimmed forevermore.
   If beauty worships Endymion's ghost,
     Yet night is but the shaded map of day
     And cannot always last, it must away,
   Then, Disappointment, thou art wretched most.

Aye! cold life-giver, circumstantial child,
   'Twere better thou wert orphaned and in hell,
     For Time's indifference differs most in thee.
Heedful too late, regardless, wild,
   But nowise vague, yet—heavy truth to tell—
     Thou art the sword in many a touchy me.
Indeed thou art not circumscribed at all;
Thy range is not of men nor wisdom small;
   Nor any too sagacious is thy creed.
     If thou wouldst in thy triumph only die,
     Oh, that were something! but thy partial eye
Can see no wound till lulling life is freed.

Death is thy victory ! nathless thy gain
   Is small enough and thou art ill repaid;
      Anticipation of reputed worth,
Itself repudiated and made plain,
   Is but a poor inheritance. Thus weighed,
      Behold thee, a degenerate of earth!
An only ruler of the blind that see,
The deaf that hear, the dumb that speak through thee.
   Then wherefore art thou vain? Then wherefore proud ?
    True, thou wert never so! true, to be sure—
    Thou couldst not be and ever thus endure,
   For pride dies young and thou art still uncowed.

Imagination, too, is of thy breed,
   And thou art sponsor for it to the end,
      For well thou knowest 'tis no foe of thine;
For well thou knowest where it sows its seed,
   Thyself doth ever faithfully attend,
      Casting thy muck along the furrowed line;
Nor canst thou be called faithless to thy trust,
Although thou art to honest faith unjust,
   Who hath not injured thee in all her days,
    Yet knew thee only to behold thee foul.
    If virtue dwelleth 'neath a friar's cowl
   Then thou art all of this in many ways.

THROCKMORTON.

Believe me, stranger, if ever lover
    Or constant rover through flowery meads,
A spirit dwells in Throckmorton's valleys
    And winding alleys of balmy reeds.

A spirit laden with faithful sorrows,
    That shames the morrow's indulgent ray;
Whereas the meadows bespeak a season
    When hearts of reason are ever gay.

But do not stay it, or rudely linger
    To lay a finger upon its shroud ;
For 'tis a maiden whose soul's in heaven,
    Whose love was given, but ne'er allowed.

Respect her mission, for she is holy
    And wanders solely with steadfast thought;
She seeks a lover who may remember
    A dead December was illy bought.

She seeks a sailor who loved the ocean
    With that devotion which feared no ill;
And this betokened an angry sire,
    Whose aim was higher and higher still.

He pined and fretted that his fair jewel
    Could be so cruel to cross his mind;
And oft he pleaded, she never trembled,
    Nor aught dissembled, for she was blind.

Her one bright loadstar, he did discover,
    Was her bold lover and nothing more.
If he reproved her, he ne'er consented,
    Nor late repented and all was o'er.

Remorse hath killed her, and earth, her mother,
　In lieu of other reclaimed its own,
And soon consigned her in snowy vestments
　Where love's assessments might ne'er be known.

Some seven summers hath passed and missed her
　Where oft they kissed her in woodland dells;
Where oft she loitered in brakes and brambles
　And lover's rambles, sighing "farewells."

But now her spirit, divine and deathless,
　All pale and breathless and ill at ease,
Is nightly haunting the lonesome passes
　And dank morasses and mossy leas.

She ofttimes pauses, where one reposes,
　Beneath the roses, blood-red in hue;
An humble headstone blotched, blurred and broken,
　Mayhap hath spoken, but nothing new.

Nathless her features express a measure
　Of earthly pleasure, of human grace;
For lo! her idol, no more a rover
　Or gentle lover, hath run his race.

Scarred Tamalpais, black-browed and hoary,
　May know his story and how he died,
But never whispers to her who nightly
　Wrongly or rightly doth near abide.

Not out of reason, tho' sins forgiven,
　She counts in heaven a world of tears;
E'er;death hath claimed her she did inherit
　This restless spirit and many fears.

LAKE MERRITT.

Upon thy banks my fancy roves
To all those sweet embroidered groves
    Of well remembered story;
And often there I lay me down
In Autumn, when the leaves are brown,
    And dream of phantom glory.

'Twas thou, blest talisman of youth,
Inspired what words of beauty's truth
    That with me are united;
And toned the lone, the love-sick days
Which first gave substance to the lays
    That worldly wisdom blighted.

Yon full-blown sails that skim the wave,
And more intrepidly doth brave
    The distant estuary,
May yield to others keen delight,
But give me shelter in thy sight
    With hearts that never vary.

These shores that line thee, marvelous lake,
Doth something of thyself partake—
    Thy whole-souled animation—
From low St. Mary's convent walls
To where the jutting roadway falls
    By easy, slow gradation.

Nor I alone doth on thee gaze
With dreamy eye and sense ablaze,
    Beyond rhyme's worthy mention,
For oft I've seen thy bordering glade
Protect the twice-protected maid
    From niggard apprehension.

And something on thy surface said,
'Twas e'er thy native beauty led
 Earth's sympathetic daughters
To pause beneath yon spreading oaks,
And vow love's sweet and tender yokes,
 Still gazing on thy waters.

Full many a Sabbath hour I played
The truant from the greater shade
 Of some stern-visaged preacher
To idly float upon thy breast,
Whilst my rapt spirit would attest
 Thou wert the better teacher;

For in thy shallow marge I viewed
The folly of ingratitude,
 The baseness of dissembling;
And oft beheld with heart-still joy,
A bold, a truly wilful boy,
 At his reflection trembling.

Nor was this least of what I learnt,
But so deep was its wisdom burnt,
 In those bright hours of leisure,
That still I feel its inward trend
Trace and retrace to some dark end
 The years it doth out-measure.

A busy life since intervened
To part the youth that from thee weaned,
 A spiritual reason;
Though still reserved within his heart
Dwelleth thy pictured counterpart
 Through change, and stress, and season.

Live on then, peaceful lake, fore'er,
Nor let one sullen churl declare
   Thy charms grow cold and colder;
Belie not this lone feeble bard,
Who loved thee with no small regard
   And in that love grew bolder.

———

MAY WAS A MONTH OF VARIED HUE.

May was a month of varied hue,
The heart tempting the eye to view
   What cold December misses.
May was—but is not any more—
A faithful friend, and all my lore
   Was smiles and sighs and kisses.

Her genial rays were gently sweet;
Her gladsome days too short to meet
   The soul's wish that grew dearer.
Yet truth, full-fledged, doth declare
The present May is just as fair,
   And to perfection nearer.

Then tell me, weak and fluttering mind,
Why are you thus to May unkind?
   Why are you thus untruthful?
What Lizzie said, thyself shoulds't say,
That never in the month of May
   Ought any heart grow ruthful.

O Lizzie ! wert thou living still,
These thoughts that deaden my weak will
  Would meet a bold dissenter;
Thy death it was that firstly called
Their substance forth, and later palled
  A somewhat vague repenter.

Between the cold and glittering stars
Mine eyes behold th' celestial bars
  That guard the gates of heaven.
Yet, tell me Fate, should I, too, die,
Will Lizzie know?   Will she be nigh?
  Will soul meet soul forgiven?

Thou glorious Light of Gethsemane!
'Tis holy custom to maintain
  That Thou wert faulty never;
And such a light was Lizzie's love,
That my soul centers it above
  Forever and forever.

O earth's emoluments!   O fame!
What can ye add unto her name
  Which she doth not inherit?
What can ye give or take away
Within this fleeting month of May
  To match her radiant spirit?

I ventured from the beaten path
  Where alien footsteps seldom tread;
And kindred man much usage hath
  The weary hours to toil for bread.

Not here, I mused, doth fancy nest;
  Too somber these decaying walls
For her abidance: here folks rest
  When laughter rings through marble halls.

I measured slow the wooden walk
  That bordered on a narrow lane,
And heard the sound of lowly talk
  Within the sound of this refrain:

"London bridge is falling down,
Falling down, falling down;
London bridge is falling down,
My——fair——lady."

My course was soon abruptly blocked
  By a cute, little circling throng
Of happy children, gingham-frocked,
  Singing that quaint, prophetic song.

I calmly, though intently, gazed
  Upon their interesting play,
At which they paused, and seemed amazed,
  But soon again resumed their lay:

"London bridge is falling down,
Falling down, falling down;
London bridge is falling down,
My——fair——Lady."

One pretty miss sat by, alone,
  The victim of some sad mistake;
And made betimes a tearful moan,
  As if her little heart would break.

I questioned her and said: " My child,
  Why sit you here, and crying, too? "
She wiped her eyes and blandly smiled,
  Half-hesitating what to do.

Again repeating my remark,
  She answered in a bashful way:
" My father went to prison, sir;
  And those girls never let me play."

With that she wept and wept aloud,
  But kindness seemed to soothe her pain;
She suffered for the dreadful cloud,
  Although it was the father's stain.

" There, little girl," I said, " don't cry,
  You shall have candy; dry your tears."
Her hand I took, and we passed by,
  Amidst the others' deafening jeers.

'Tis thus, the parents' sins descend
  Upon the inoffensive child—
O heaven, spare a reckless end,
  To one thus wrongfully exiled.

Not only doth distinctions dwell
  Among the higher walks of life;
The smallest babe may live to tell
  Of discord sprung from simple strife.

That journey then, shall I repent?
   Nay! something to the hour I owe;
The child, the fate she underwent,
   Those words oft through my mind yet flow.

What they portend, I may not tell;
   Time works its wonders many ways!
Yet one lone voice I cannot quell,
   Forever and anon it says:

"London bridge is falling down,
Falling down, falling down;
London bridge is falling down,
My——fair——lady."

———

SONG.

Sigh not, fair maid! Oh, sigh not so!
   'Twill ne'er relieve thy inmost pain;
Thy trusting heart can never know
   Sweet joy again, sweet joy again.
Life's hopes, ere Love a truant turned,
   Are blasted now and borne away;
The heart wherein its fervor burned
   Must turn to clay, must turn to clay.

FERDINAND TO MEDORA.*

I.

Thy rolling orbs I gazed upon but once—
Once fairly in the dim, unnatural past;
Yet it sufficed, and brought forth quick response
Of love, more bountiful than any blast
From the foul mouth of Beelzebub. Upon
Thy bosom I could lay my head for aye
In peaceful slumber. Oh! what holy Don
Could fain do else or any charm gainsay.
I might outlive Methusaleh of old,
   If thou wouldst smile on me one even hour
With that felicity which doth unfold
   More passion than which any regal dower
Is merest garbage, sickening to behold,
   And like the scourge which doth fair earth deflower.

II.

God made thee for a purpose, and I own
   'Twas some such mission as the birds confide
To ears acute, whose notes are oft implied
As voices from the Maker's august throne.
No beauty can I gage thee to; no zone
   Can from its earth such nourishment provide
To yield its children that which is denied
By lassitude and granted thee alone.
O thou, clay's choicest clay! eternal spring!
   Beacon of sanctity! bright star of man!
Where'er thou treadest, chaos stalks behind,
Making life's wisdom seem a poisoned sting,
   The sage's years a little eclipsed span,
   And this vast universe a thing divined.

* The following sonnets are supposed to have been written by a man out of
sympathy with his time and the qualities of his fellow-man. Presumably, one who
held honor to be no sin; yet it cannot be denied that he sometimes exhausts his own
patience and occasionally takes a fling at the "eternal verities." But whether this
was the intent of his desire, or the unconsciousness of cynicism, it matters little.
Few can master the intricacies of love, much less define its vagaries, seeing it is no
child of judgment.

III.

Alas! I envy the absorbent sun
  That lights thy chamber in the early morn,
And drinks thy pregnant beauty in as one,
  Intoxicated by a drug forsworn.
I envy not the dawn which loves my love,
  I only envy that which, lost to me,
May something richer to the bearer prove,
  And leave me helpless with mad jealousy.
      If 'twere some mortal wight I fain would vow
        An everlasting hatred to the same;
      And stamp malignity upon his brow,
        So all the world would know him "thief" by
          name.
  For who so robs me profits wrongful gain,
  And leaves me an insolvent's direful stain.

IV.

Betimes I linger on thy happy words
  That flow like honey from thy servant tongue.
Oh ! they are precious omens like the birds
  That starred the heavens when great poets sung;
Something of light and shadow doth they leave,
  Something which mine own confidence calls love.
Yet, tell me not that they in this deceive,
  Or that my fancy will but fancy prove.
      May nothing surfeit me to mine own ill,
        Except that which love can alone sustain,
      By the mere action of thy present will,
        Whose everything is light to this refrain;
      For thou canst shame to death my weaker years,
      And their fine phantasy of boding fears.

V.

The thought was tender when the night was long,
  That when the morrow broke I would unfold
To thy half-clos'ed ears a plaintive song,
  Sung oft these thousand years by knights of old.
No fear or thought of fear dwelt in my heart—
  Nothing but pleasant memories—when day,
All spank and rosy, drew its lids apart,
  And blushed to find me on the open way.
    O day ! blot out thy cold transparencies !
      O night ! heart's revenue to thee I yield !
    Friend of desire and keeper of the keys
      Of promise, day hath shamefully concealed.
    I must have sunshine, yet day be my night,
    Night day, sun moon, moon sun, and darkness light.

VI.

Men taught me knowledge, but I learnt it not.
  You taught me love and I learned wisdom, too.
  Behold the paradox !   This residue
Of love is wisdom's heritage: begot
From judgment's loins by strategy and plot.
  Therefore whatever sequences ensue,
  I am the debtor, for I owe to you
More than dependent years can e'er outblot.
  My little virtue is out-virtued twice,
    And fretting days are oft subordinate
  To my mind's will; but by no sacrifice
    Of love's own divertisements, which create
  A gradual evolution in my soul,
  Half-halving half, yet one continuous whole.

VII.

The lights of seven centuries grow pale,
  When beauty's substance 'fore me doth arise;
And all my years seem voiceless; and I fail
  For words to spread the transports of mine eyes.
Though these dead gods of my idolatry,
  Give voice to wisdom and sweet tunes to thought;
It falls on stony ears.   O ecstasy!
    O love ! thy joys—how dearly are they bought.
      Yet he is rich who can forget the cares
        Which wisdom gives: for beauty's self inspires
      A keener love than knowledge ever shares—
        A sweeter truth, Medora, than the fires
      Of all the masters.   Be it ever so !
      They first must love who would true wisdom know.

VIII.

If I grow riotous with early love,
  And sooner languish in the world's decay,
Thyself art ever sweetening some fair grove,
  Whose greater greatness never fades away.
Not an enchantress would I argue thee,
  Nor an immortal with a sibyl's voice;
Though thy bright soul is purer than the sea,
  Yet thou art still of earth; in that rejoice.
    Love blinds the eye and lends an angel's grace,
      To simple maidens void of beauty's art.
    But thou dost need no love to give thee place,
      Still it were meet, love should control thy heart.
    Now vow to press me further to this point,
    And I will show thee great worlds out of joint.

IX.

To paint the virtues of a given soul,
  Whose radiance glows like the first touch of day,
Is far beyond my pow'r.   Mine is a role
  Wholly removed from fancy gently gay.
Hence, failure may be written on my brow,
  And all the fury of a South-sea storm
May rage within me, but I cannot now,
  Nor any time, such offices perform.
    Thou fain would earless be to this discourse,
      Lest it should lend thee an assuming air;
    Yet truth will out, and with it the remorse,
      That cannot one without the other share.
    'Twere folly to be wise, if 'twere ordained
    That wit with beauty unholy war maintained.

X.

Thy spiritual self is wed with mine,
  Indifferent to thy heart's material strains,
  Nor with what tone its hollow voice complains.
In close embrace, oft hath I lain supine,
Sipping thy spirit love—O love divine !—
  From mellifluous lips, whose touch enchains,
  Like Virtue's loadstar.   In such holy fanes
My own soul's unity is lost in thine.
    The very essences of mundane joy
      Are dregs to this pure wine of revery—
      This etherealism.   Canst thou deny
    That thy love's spirit is mine to employ,
      In whatsoever fashion I may deem—
      Since things are what they are, not what they seem ?

XI.

Upon the fading vision of each day
    With sweet excess of sadness I do mourn,
When thou, fair soul, doth to thy kindred stray,
    Making dear hardships for a soul doubt-torn.
Not to the eye perceptible the pain;
    Not to the ear perceptible the sound;
Yet instinct and its subtle sense makes plain,
    Prophetic fear of an approaching wound.
        Oh, may the thought be brother to the fear,
            As illegitimate, as fatherless,
        And far less conscientious, far less dear.
            But wishing cannot drown or kill distress:
        For on a hill, where twenty spruce-trees grow,
        Some immemorial spring abides below.

XII.

Test not the merit of my love by day,
    Nor judge me by man's dull prosaic wit:
    None but thyself hath ever fashioned it,
None, e'en thyself, can doom it to decay.
The narrow rut of life hath lost its sway,
    And to the future I shall oft commit
    What vestiges of love as best seem fit
To lend effulgence to imperfect clay.
    My life in resignation is confined,
        Like drooping lilies where no bud reposes,
            And these rehearsals fitting food for thought.
    Time's interstices thereby are inclined
        As the apprentice to what God discloses,
            Showing simplicity in what was sought.

XIII.

Rather seek calmer judgment in the night,
  When glorious stars add luster to the scene;
And their tranquillity sheds softer light
  O'er thy soul's pathway: then convene
  Whatever witnesses may come between
The error and the virtue of my right.
  And let thy senses resolutely glean
In one small moment what the years recite.
  Deal gently with my faults, for they are much,
    And weigh more heavily upon my mind,
      Than that great pressure of the keener air,
  Round some high altitude. And pray give touch
  To what I mean to be, and be as blind
    To what I am, as best may speak thee fair.

XIV.

Thy servants prosper nobly at thy will,
  Sharing a richer heritage than I;
They see thee daily, see thee to their fill,
  Whilst to myself that vantage you deny.
Thy lowest minion hath me on the hip,
  Being a very spoilsman of that touch,
Which doth all nature change, at one fell slip,
  And thus, and thus my love limps on a crutch.
  Each moment moves me further from my stand,
    And crowds me close and closer to the wall;
  Each new despair is like a swelling gland
    That soon must burst and bring an end to all.
  Whatever moveth hearts, I know it not;
  But this I know: my love is quite forgot.

XV.

Wert thou by nature preordained to grant
    Reprisals to the scriveners of time,
Oh! how the very tongues of men would pant,
    Singing thy orisons in ev'ry clime.
There is more subject-matter in thine eyes,
    Whose concentrated wealth is vaster far
Than all the pure, beseeming gold that lies
    In Sirius, the great, the mighty star.
      Give then the promise which those eyes withhold,
        That the fulfilment may seem nothing strange.
      Writing (fair oracle) is purer gold,
        Than speech, which may by situation change;
      Leaving a void unbridged, a noxious fear,
      A love unwholesome, or a barren year.

XVI.

Why comest not the question to thy mind
    That needs must seek an answer at its birth?
Am I vainglorious, or thou unkind,
    To read my humor as a cause for mirth?
Were my inquiry to the haughty breed,
    These hopes were surely barren of returns;
And to them all I would their all concede,
    But this from thee most inhumanely burns.
      Oh, could I have foreseen what now is plain,
        This busy tongue of mine were long since stilled
      In golden silence. This then to my gain:
        I have been civil when my passion willed
      A fiery eloquence. But it was fate
      That I, alas, should love a lass too late.

XVII.

Though for itself truth needs no advocate,
  Nor man's indorsement for its current note.
Yet who shall say what's truth ?   And who shall state
  This man or that learned not his truth by rote
And therefore is a weakling 'fore the fact ?
  Since, by comparison, he'll truth declare,
While truth itself is in itself intact,
  And needs must stand or fall by its own wear.
    Yet this is truth: when I say truth is love,
      That's truth's full measurement and nothing less;
    And thou, sweet truth, who art the soul thereof,
      (Love being truth, truth love) why, I profess,
    What's in the soul of ev'ry eye to see:
    Hence, by this sign let all truth judged be.

XVIII.

Gilding report and making it seem sweet
  To Time's advantage and my lady's ear
  Will find in me no steward, for I fear
Love's introspection may be incomplete,
And thereby first-born promises defeat.
  Mayhap some lamer makeshift I hold dear
  With less of reason than doth here appear;
If so, denial cannot say, 'tis meet.
    While day and night are kin to one another,
      They are not less at variance for the same;
    Both have designs; each one upon the other,
      And reason nothing, being lost to shame.
    Therefore report, which I hath oft foresworn
    By silence, may be otherwise than scorn.

XIX.

To blush were to admit unreasoned facts,
    And stand self-wilted in the eyes of men,
To whom I'll not confess my secret acts,
    Since love's true parts seem ill within their ken;
But rather passion, nameth after love,
    Bearing a foul injustice in the name.
Therefore, the grace of Providence above,
    And thy apology I humbly claim.
        Yet, ask me not cold, borrowed looks to wear,
            When I must wear them with a low conceit,
        Against all virtue.   Love, as thou art fair,
            As thou art noble, honorable, sweet,
        I swear I'll not deny, if I'm accused,
        That I was half a hundred times refused !

XX.

The month, the day, the hour, and the event,
    Hath chorused happily this endless song
And stereotyped its curious argument
    By persuasion and a living wrong.
If Poverty will of its own complain,
    Then I, like usurers, defend my trade;
Though this may gather little to my gain,
    Yet I of little, little am afraid.
        In this acknowledgment you nothing lose,
            Since nothing is acknowledged by thy voice;
        And whatsoever mood thou mayest choose,
            By me is comprehended virtue's choice.
        Thus in this paradoxal world I stand,
        An Atlas with a crutch in either hand.

XXI.

Who is this upstart that doth soil thy name
  By offering to the public eye his notes?
His treachery may warrant him a fame
  Of precious nothings, for on love he dotes;
And love, these lamentations can attest,
  Is a too-feeble borrower of wit.
But mark his stubbornness; what he confessed
  Must wrench a heart that's proud there's pride in it.
    Yea! do him justice. He loves beauty first,
      And where its creed is best exemplified
    He pays high court. Oh, what a noble thirst!
      If he were silent long he must of died.
    Indeed, Time wrongs him, for he meant no ill,
    And honored patience with a right good will.

XXII.

O sweet felicity! O gentle song!
  Why art thou so reticent? Why so strange?
Like some coy maiden who hath loved full long
  And wed desire marveled at her change.
So marvel I, Medora, at the range
  Love plays its tunes in; so have I oft wept
Full many hours in life's vacuous grange,
  Till in the arms of Morpheus I slept,
And sleeping dreamt and dreaming dreamt in vain—
  Thou art my one religion and the priest
  Of ev'ry hope that inwardly doth feast
With love, and love will ever thus remain
  To rouse a smoldering passion to a fire
  That burns beyond conception and desire.

XXIII.

I may not live to prosecute my bent,
  Making sweet sounds and discords with one breath:
For if thy heart refuse thy lips consent,
  My speech is ended: silence then and death.
This cumbersome existence will not fear
  The all too-dreaded specter nor his train,
But love more patiently the new-born year,
  That claims my own dénouement to thy gain.
    Distinctions, nor the partial bonds of hope,
      Are not less gaged by any of thy clan.
    Indeed, I would more willingly elope
      With all thy wishes, if they were of man,
    Than here remain to color with remorse,
    That part of thee which love cannot indorse.

XXIV.

Build me no cenotaph when my last breath
  Makes but a faint impression on the glass!
What this small life hath oft encountereth
  Is monument enough: so let it pass.
If thou alone shouldst fittingly survive
  In thy heart's heart love's faithful love confide—
My little all—keep only that alive,
  And it shall bloom like that which never died.
    'Twill vie in perfect beauty with the rose,
      That patiently awaits the dewy morn.
    Not as the quivering stream that onward flows
      To the uncertain sea; not as the thorn
    That secret lurks in summer's fairest flower
    And consecrates with blood its nuptial hour.

XXV.

This simple song ne'er had a preface to it,
  And by these signs 'twill never have an end;
Nor I, nor any part of me will rue it,
  What loves designs I surely will commend.
However, may my judgment err in singing,
  The subject is infallible, 'tis plain;
My fault with me will die, while thou art bringing
  To ages love, therein will lie the gain.
    Therefore, no truth's apology I owe,
      To life, love, immortality or death;
    Therefore, I will not anything bestow,
      Excepting that which thou hast given breath.
    These simples even heaven will respect,
    For God is love's unerring architect.

XXVI.

Judge me not by my looks ! Believe me, dear,
  My pen is weak-kneed to the thoughts that stray
  Their everlasting sanguinary way
Throughout my throbbing brain. I dread with fear
The spectacle of those that volunteer
  To yield me small advantage, yet betray
  Whatever confidence I might display
By any deed acknowledged in the clear.
  Could I half signify what in thee lies,
    Or paint the fringes of thy glorious lights
  With truth's own pencil—these, my soulfelt sighs,
    Could not attest the joy born in such rites.
  Thou, love, may'st even shut thy sensate eyes,
    But think not man can e'er attain those heights.

XXVII.

Religiously I scan those lesser stars
  That burn their silent watchfires in the sky,
In bold defiance to the warlike Mars,
  Whose malice is all patent to the eye.
In them I see the likeness of my love,
  Willing to grant, but fearing aught to give;
Courting forbearance for the sake thereof,
  When that sweet excellence in her doth live.
    So with this very grace that fears dispraise
      Is measured out to me a fickle faith
    That dies bewitched. Oh! when love's devious ways
      Are horoscoped, 'tis then that Nature saith:
    What mischief love and love alone will cause
    By mocking happy and consistent laws.

XXVIII.

If I have dared to love thee, 'tis enough;
  I'll dare no more! To some, that were a sin
No penance could absolve. Yet, to such stuff
  As wits call love, it is more pure within
Than drifted snow. Oh! rob me not of chance
  To prove it thus, or I am dead indeed.
Pray give it hope, and some small circumstance,
  And it will shame the thought that bore it seed
And bless the soul it worships. Bear with it,
  Nor close thine ears when it would voice its worth.
If it lack opportunity and wit
  'Twill be fore'er a vulgar thing of earth,
From which no deed immortal may arise
To brave the power of the utmost skies.

XXIX.

When I make merry with a passive soul,
  Pray see me with no penetrating eye;
For there the loss.   In many a shallow role
  I oft laugh outward, with an inward sigh.
But truth's a verity, and thou art truth—
  What I may be is little to my mind;
Youth is a golden star, and thou art youth,
  To whose fair light is everything inclined.
    Not my enlargement nor the unknown world
      Beyond the misty courses of renown
    Can make me else; and what is here unfurled
      Is passion-painted, without jest or frown.
    But these, my hopes, are built on such loose earth
    That this transcription shows a woeful dearth.

XXX.

Away dull care ! and all thy fears away !
  Go thou and nestle in a royal skull,
  And thou wilt find in poor discernment's full
Great measure sleeping through a witless day.
Hence, beauty shall inspire me, and I'll say
  I was to beauty featureless and dull,
  But am what beauty can no more annul
Than pardon.   Therefore, may I not be gay!
  But hold a bit :   Is this that self-same me
    That swore my love to ev'ry first-born rose ?
  O, God forgive! if true timidity
    Should blush to murmur it ; and thus it goes:
  So, love, be generous, and my song ill-sung,
  Will still be debtor to a poet's tongue.

XXXI.

Those bald distinctions which grow poor with age
　　I never craved, and thou dost know it well.
Not with imported airs I'll blot this page,
　　Nor with false luster win thee by a spell;
I'll be as plain as any poet dare,
　　And still be poet to his understanding.
All things I'll hazard, nothing will I spare,
　　To live in humbleness at thy commanding.
　　　　Knowing thy taste gains little in those creeds,
　　　　　Which most find favor in the public eye,
　　　　I am resigned.   If, then, my love succeeds,
　　　　　Its laurels are its own, and signify
　　That love is ne'er disqualified for long,
　　Though error hath a reason for its wrong.

XXXII.

No, never, on my honor as a man,
　　Will I presume to have grown gravely wise
In humblest judgment.   'Tis the better plan:
　　Time hath more shifts than most men realize.
By this I aim no slander at thy sex;
　　I only know what I've misunderstood
And thought least likely.   If my actions vex
　　The soul of man, why, it is well they should.
　　　　With this uncertainty before my face
　　　　　I still see virtue where she ever dwelt—
　　　　In thee, Medora—of thee, of thy race,
　　　　　Before whose holy altar have I knelt
　　Heart-lonely, undetermined, in a spell,
　　Where I beheld things I shall never tell.

XXXIII.

I late beheld an Oriental dame,
  Decked in the gorgeous splendor of her race.
She sang of love, of chivalry, of fame,
  With harmony untold and matchless grace.
Her style was native and the touch she used
  Was something marvelously rare, indeed ;
Also, a deathless spirit she infused,
  Made ev'ry heart with mutual pity bleed.
    Methinks a love-lorn look was in her eyes,
      Which spoke a slavish inference to me;
    But I was cold to her hot-blooded sighs,
      (For hath I not of love sufficiency?)
    And with a Spartan courage looked her bold,
    Whom I conceived to have a heart of gold.

XXXIV.

Things mutable and curiously strange
  Are bosom friends to me and my complaint;
Indeed, I marvel at the interchange
  Of their dumb hospitality, and faint
With mighty wonderment ; whenas, the eye
  Of my inherent self doth gaze within
And notes a motley phalanx passing by,
  Whose charitable grace burns deep my sin.
    Thou marvelest, yet much needs be forgiven
      'Ere substance to its proper shade is suited
    To make love seem a stepping-stone to heaven,
      Where honor nor dishonesty is bruited.
    So, gentle augurer, do read awhile
    The chart of love—may pity make thee smile.

XXXV.

While those twin stars that glisten 'neath thy brow
  Are still life-givers of a world of light
And laws metrical, I am e'er, as now,
  A lone apostle wandering in the night.
While this is so (which seems forever so),
  All is not darkness, tho' the sultry sun
Hath faded from my heart. I come, I go,
  A living spokesman of a race unrun.
    Despair knows nothing, and conceit knows well
      Despair knows nothing : therefore, to despair
    Were cheaply bought, and cheaply bought to sell,
      While love is dearer coming from the fair,
    To fair well-giv'n. O! compass this and say,
    To-morrow thou wilt give thy heart away.

XXXVI.

When this sad panic of Dismay doth cease,
  To yield me its unwelcome revenue,
  Then will I fly these beaten paths, nor rue,
The transformation born of such release.
Some strange presentiment hath I that Peace,
  With greater measure, will unfold to view
  Those paradisian groves where Phœbus drew
From his fair goddess such a rare increase.
    Yet still be kind to this immoderate tongue,
      Vernacular and of a minor key,
    That sings dwarfed songs 'twere better left unsung,
      And oft are limited to such degree
    That thou would'st fain some worthy note perceive,
    Who more were gratified to else believe.

XXXVII.

O, how unkind are these my thoughts to me
  That make me seem more bitter than I feel,
  Less hopeful than I am. If they doth steal
Love's earn'ed income, can'st thou therefore see
My truer self is silent tho' it be
  Impatient justly: eager to appeal,   .
  And yet still silent. Did'st I not oft kneel
And pray to love, this fact were plain to thee.
    O, stubborn heart! O, thing of trust unplaced!
      How camest thou to struggle amongst men?
    Thy thoughts were dreams, thy love was double-
      faced,
      And truth seemed variable in thy ken.
    A beast of burden, thou, unsexed, unsouled;
    A wanton that hath nursed a love for gold.

XXXVIII.

Still lives the love of seven summers sweet,
  Rosy and redolent with its first light;
Still lives the hope, whose solitary beat,
  Perpetually swings from left to right.
Think not that any moment gone were base,
  Insipid, or a scavenger of Time.
Nay, lady! I could tell thee to thy face
  What lies ill-woven in the cloth of rhyme.
    But 'tis not meet, and, lacking thy consent,
      I am subservient to deeds ill-done.
    O! couldst thou catch their flavor or my bent,
      I would rest easy with each setting sun;
    For each to-morrow were a thing of joy
    Which yesterday's comparison would cloy.

XXXIX.

Being thyself, and being nothing more,
    Then thou art nothing short of fabled Venus.
Being myself, unskilled in cunning lore,
    How can I brook the stops that come between us?
Nor will I be a truant to my love,
    To open out a path for its neglect;
Tho' time may tempt me, I shall aim to prove
    That I in love would fain be circumspect.
      Immortal wisdom gave me this desire,
        And human reason cannot take its measure,
      I love thee! and what my love doth require
        I'll give, and give it with an honest pleasure.
      Renown is dead, that was an ape of fashion,
      But love will live fore'er, the noblest passion.

XL.

Reckless am I who hath no star to guide me,
    No precedent to light my wayward course;
Love scorns me, his caresses are denied me,
    Therefore am I fit subject for remorse.
    Will no one tell me why I lack the force
To hurl his studied insults in his face?
    'Tis evident that barren is the source
Of his mock sympathy and feigned grace.
      Yet, none will dare! what folly to presume!
        If any should I would not listen to them.
      Words ofttimes wear the habitudes of doom,
        And are no sooner said than said we rue them.
      To live not 'neath some wisdom or restraint
      Bespeaks a mad sad regency and taint.

XLI.

Thou in thy beauty lookest down upon me,
 But not with pride, for humble is thy bearing.
Oh! it is well that thou shouldst frown upon me,
 For who am I, that art thy humor daring?
Thou sweetest rose that doth forever bloom!
Thy heart is rich and virtue is thy dower;
Then turn not thus away! let love's perfume
Give half its essence and 'tis still a flower.
 The nightingale, that sings its plaintive song
 In God's still hours, is not more sad than I.
 The cuckoo, with her wandering note and long,
 Hath some sweet echo which my words deny.
 Yet, while proud, high-born kinsmen pay thee court,
 I live a yoeman in thy hearts' report.

XLII.

Pray, what are names to thoughts which have no names?
 Simply a bare reflection, nothing more;
They mark distinction, though the sound defames
 Its inspiration to the very core.
Indeed, my tongue will parley with the truth,
 And give itself the lie if needs it must.
What matters it? 'tis but a trick of youth,
 And yearlings suffer nothing from the just.
 Moreover, this same birthright, called love's own,
 Is all of thine to give or take at will.
 If thou dost sin, why 'tis a luckless bone
 That chokes repentance to its utmost fill!
 Indifference may coin a right true word;
 But wouldst thou condescend it should be heard?

XLIII.

However be it in the mind of man—
  However their great luster dims mine own,
The cause is simple, for I ever ran
  In most uneven pathways to love's throne.
Some great moon-madness touched me in my sleep,
  And daylight robbed all sweetness from my soul.
I strove and floundered in the dismal deep,
  Yet ne'er withheld mine eyes from one faint goal.
    With this, the one reminder, were the end
      Perversely nigh, I'd chronicle a tale
    That every still-born waif could comprehend,
      Haunting the depths of purgatory's vale;
    And prove to these skilled wizards of the earth
    That love is nobler than a titled birth.

XLIV.

I am not rich in any moral mood,
  For honesty will never hide its face,
Which oft I do.   Call it ingratitude,
  Or what you will, for I have not the grace
To beam upon thee like a new-set star,
  That pales to insignificance the sun.
Yet let not this confession be a bar
  To opportunity with will undone.
    The single circle of an autumn day
      Hath entities which man will never guess,
    But they will die, and dying fade away,
      Like some great impulse, heavy in distress.
    Time lays the corner-stone whereon is reared
    The monumental perfidy it feared.

LINES WRITTEN TO A LADY ABOUT TO ENTER
A CONVENT.

Most virtuous lady, may I kiss thy gown,
 To show how reverently I hold the law
 That can transform thee, without speck or flaw,
From earth's mock habitude? Yet look not down
On this cold, heartless hemisphere, nor frown
 At the malignity of man. Withdraw
 The stings of high-heeled vanity and awe,
Self-doting dizzards, to some fair renown.
 O gracious lady! cloister not thy love
  In some dark structure, secret and apart
 From erring impulse. Let the lights above
  Shine in their glory, but first through thy heart;
 For sanctity like thine can win from wrong
 Man's animosity that lives life-long.

SONG.

I know not why, yet still it seems
 Since first I saw thee smiling,
I'm dwelling in a maze of dreams,
 My heart my soul beguiling.

Thy many charms and winsome ways,
 And condescensions granted,
Hath brightened my unhappy days,
 And made earth seem enchanted.

Oh, may these roseate views still hold,
 No pulsive mood e'er swerving,
Like that stanch Rock of Ages bold,
 The restless sea unnerving.

MARCUS AURELIUS ANTONINUS.

Aurelius, thou man of men,
  Of moralists, indeed, sublime;
A greater than "what might have been,"
  And spirit of all time.

No naked fact in thee was lame,
  Who first of man loved man the first;
And all the influence of fame
  Quenched not truth's heav'n-born thirst.

Deaf wert thou to earth's echoing din,
  And well the sluggish Tiber knows
Thou wert a hater of all sin,
  And soother of all wos.

A warrior within a priest,
  Whose quiet, unpretentious skill
Subdued the savage of the East,
  Remaining human still.

Rome placed upon thy head a crown,
  Which lent thee no presumptuous air;
Rome found thee still without a frown,
  And all the world was fair.

The emperor was still the man;
  The man was still an artless child,
Whom Virtue premised as she ran
  Her narrow path and wild.

BECAUSE!

Because another failed to speak his mind,
  Must I be silent too?
Because another lagged and lolled behind,
  Have I naught else to do?

Because the great truths throbbing in one's breast
  Forever and a day,
Meet, in their utterance, a blatant jest,
  Must it be so alway?

Because a lack of ready-ripened wit,
  To form a well-turned phrase,
Is else denied me, must I idly sit
  And scoff at Hermes' gaze?

If such is life, 'tis but a living death
  In one ignobly born;
A slavish birthright, or a poisoned breath,
  And earns a brother's scorn.

Therefore, begone! unrecompensive mood;
  Henceforth I know thee not;
Nor fear thee, thou base scullion, or thy rood,
  Thou filterer of rot!

Welcome the cheer that Nature hath about her;
  Welcome the sweet-toned voice
Of lovely woman; tell me not, without her,
  A true heart can rejoice.

Welcome a sister's confidence, a mother's
  Sincerity and light;
Welcome a father's watchfulness, a brother's
  Extended hand at night.

Welcome abiding constancy and love,
  Born of a faithful trust;
Welcome great truth, inspired and above
  A lean and hungry lust.

Welcome the perfect days of Summer-time,
  And all the joys they bring;
Welcome the jingle of a simple rhyme,
  Which only children sing.

On land and sea some known yet unknown voice
  Invigorates my soul;
The myrmidon within me hath no choice,
  For I am now heart-whole.

So would I always be, but truth to tell,
  I fear to-morrow's sun
Will bring the shadow that I know too well,
  And all my days are done.

The melancholy blight is with me still—
  Still spiteful as of yore ;
I cannot shed it, for it hath a will,
  And knows me to the core.

Nor do I longer marvel at its touch ;
  It comes like an old friend
That knew me once and knew me over-much,
  Still knowing to the end.

If then this liberty is dearly bought,
  Its substance is more sweet,
And like the hind that lacks a human thought,
  Will swallow its defeat.

But while the humor lives I'll spread my nets
  Beyond the Farallones,
Where hoary Neptune daily fumes and frets,
  Making his constant moans.

And when the humor dies I'll back to land,
  And jostle with the crowd ;
And few will know and fewer understand
  Why one man spoke aloud.

www.ingramcontent.com/pod-product-compliance
Lightning Source LLC
Chambersburg PA
CBHW020226090426
42735CB00010B/1600